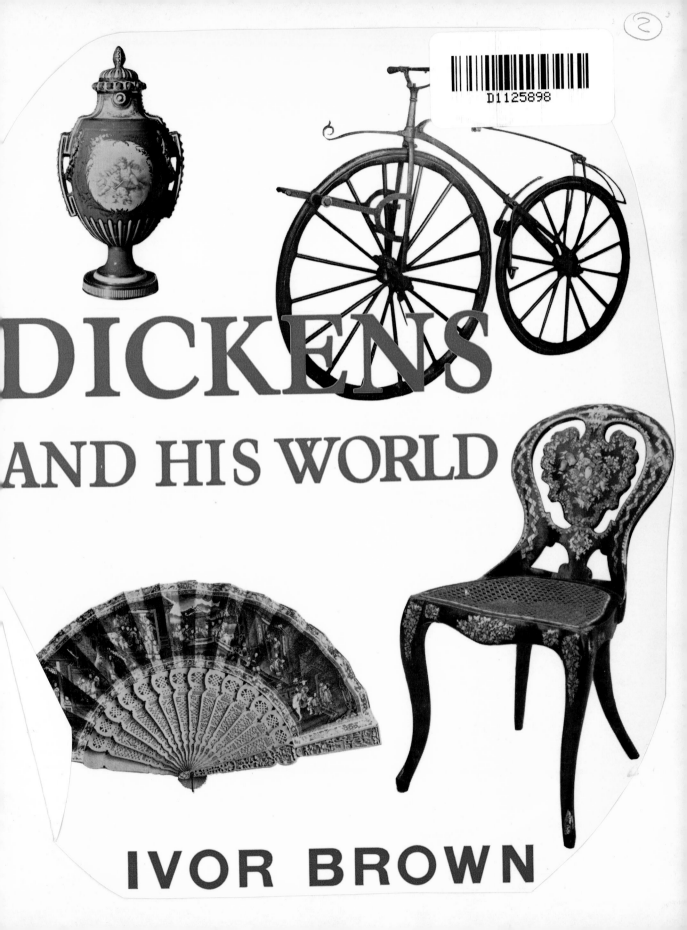

DICKENS
AND HIS WORLD

IVOR BROWN

DICKENS
AND HIS WORLD

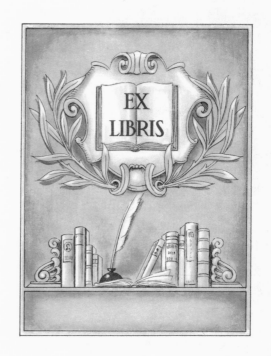

A cut glass ink bottle used by Dickens in his study
at Gad's Hill.

Gustave Doré's engraving of a London slum in the 1870s. The squalid houses are huddled back to back and a viaduct carries the smoke and filth of the railways right into the heart of town.

DICKENS
AND HIS WORLD

IVOR BROWN

*Author of "Shakespeare
and His World", "Dr.
Johnson and His World",
and "Jane Austen and
Her World".*

LUTTERWORTH PRESS · LONDON

Acknowledgements

The Publishers wish to thank the following for permission to reproduce photographs of which they hold the copyright. The numbers in brackets refer to the pages on which they appear: Portsmouth City Museums [1, 6]; Mansell Collection [2, 7, 9, 21, 23, 36 (upper), 37 (upper)]; National Portrait Gallery [5, 10, 12, 13, 19, 30]; The Trustees of the Dickens House [8 (upper), 48]; Barnaby's Picture Library [8 (lower), 16, 18]; The Victoria and Albert Museum Crown Copyright [11, 14 (lower), 15, 34]; reproduced by gracious permission of Her Majesty the Queen [14 (upper)]; Radio Times Hulton Picture Library [20, 22, 24, 25, 33, 39, 40 (right)]; London Museum [26 (left), 32, 35 (lower), 38]; British Museum [26 (right), 35 (upper)]; Crown Copyright, Science Museum, London [27]; Photo., Science Museum, London [28 (lower), 29]; Museum of British Transport, Clapham [28 (upper), 30 (lower)]; Photo., London Transport [31]; Gallery of English Costume, City of Manchester Art Galleries [36 (lower), 37 (lower)]; Cheltenham Ladies' College [40 (left)]; Rugby School [41]; Illustrated London News [42, 43, 45 (lower)]; National Army Museum [44, 45 (upper), 46]; Australian News and Information Bureau [47].

CHARLES DICKENS, the eldest son of John Dickens, a clerk in the Navy Pay Office, was born at Portsmouth on February 7, 1812, the second of eight children. His father's work was transferred to London two years later and to Chatham in the county of Kent in 1817. The family stayed there for five years, during which the boy was well taught at the school of Mr. Giles and was an eager reader at home. He became devoted to Kent with its shipping on the Medway, its orchards, and its coaches on the roads with the clatter of hoofs and sounding of horns, and he never forgot it. His last home, Gad's Hill, was there and so was the setting of his last and unfinished book, *The Mystery of Edwin Drood*.

Back in London in 1822, the family had hard times to face. Dickens's father got himself into serious debt. In an attempt to earn some money Mrs. Dickens tried to keep a school, but this was a total failure. John Dickens, having failed to repay the money he owed, was arrested and sent to Marshalsea Prison in Southwark, and his wife and the younger children went with him, which was the normal procedure in those days. Charles, then aged twelve, went to work long, hungry hours in a dingy and rat-ridden blacking factory. After three months John Dickens was able to discharge his debt from a small legacy he received and Charles returned to school. However, he never forgot the drudgery and humiliation of this episode and made use of his unhappy experiences in *David Copperfield*, just as life in a debtor's prison as he had seen it was described in his other novels, especially in *The Pickwick Papers* and *Little Dorrit*.

5

THE HARD, PORTSEA.

The Hard, Portsea, as it must have looked when Dickens's father was a clerk in the Portsmouth dockyard. Though the family moved away when Dickens was only two, he could remember the garden of their house at Portsea.

A wooden paper knife which belonged to Dickens.

At fifteen Charles Dickens left school and became an office-boy, and then a clerk in lawyers' offices, where he came to despise the delays, stupidities and cruelties of the legal system. He taught himself shorthand and in 1832 began working in the press gallery of the House of Commons. His reputation for energy and accuracy was high and that was enhanced when he worked from 1833 to 1835 as a journalist, both reporting the proceedings of the House of Commons and making long journeys by coach into country towns to bring back accounts of important political speeches, work that gave him a lasting contempt for politicians.

He spent his time away from Parliament in watching his fellow-Londoners in their recreations, their work and their poverty. These were brilliantly described in his first book *Sketches by Boz* (1836). This led to a publisher's commission to write "a book of sporting adventures" which would be published not as a book but as a series of instalments which the public could buy, month by month, as they appeared. The first number appeared in 1836 and was entitled *The Posthumous Papers of the Pickwick Club*. This was very well received by the readers, and his reputation and the sales rose rapidly after the introduction of Mr. Pickwick's man-servant Sam Weller in the fifth instalment. Dickens could now afford to marry. He and his bride, Kate Hogarth, lived at first in Doughty Street, Bloomsbury, now Dickens House, a small museum open to visitors. Needing more space for a growing family he later moved to larger and more fashionable houses, first in Devonshire Place and then in Tavistock Square.

In 1838 Dickens was at work on *Nicholas Nickleby* and travelled north to investigate the scandal of the Yorkshire Schools, on one of whose owners he based the monstrous, and perhaps exaggerated, figure of the headmaster, Squeers. Success was immediate. So was that of *The Old Curiosity Shop*. In 1841 he had the signal honour of being granted at the age of twenty-nine the Freedom of the City of Edinburgh. America followed Scotland in acclamation. With his wife he crossed the Atlantic in 1842 and after a warm

6

welcome roused some bitter enmity by his criticism of American life in *American Notes*. This was increased when great offence was caused by the American episodes in *Martin Chuzzlewit*, appearing in 1843, in which Martin is involved in the fraudulent affair of the new city of Eden.

His energy was unquenchable. From 1844 to 1847 he travelled in Europe, took the editor's chair of a new London paper, *The Daily News*, became an amateur actor, lectured, wrote *The Christmas Carol* and other Christmas books and started work on *Dombey and Son*. In 1849 *David Copperfield*, his autobiographical novel, began to appear in sections. He said that it was his own favourite book and it has been his most widely popular. In the following year he became Editor of a weekly magazine, *Household Words*, to which he contributed largely while recruiting other eminent writers.

Amid all these labours he enjoyed Victorian society and was an active supporter and speaker for many philanthropic causes. He continued his journeys in Europe while working on *Bleak House*. He collected the material for *Hard Times*, published in 1854, in the textile manufacturing towns of Lancashire, and then began *Little Dorrit*. In 1856 he bought a property called Gad's Hill in Kent, near Rochester, where he settled for the rest of his life.

Enjoying his power as an actor, he began in 1859 to give dramatic readings of extracts from his works, and won and enjoyed great success on the platform. The journeys and fatigues involved did not interrupt his writing. Before 1865 he had published *A Tale of Two Cities* and *Our Mutual Friend*. His health deteriorated after a severe shock in a railway accident, but that did not deter him from a second visit to America in 1867–68, where his readings were immensely successful and the old dislike of him was swamped in a new and friendly admiration. Though physically weakening, he continued his dramatic readings and also began work on a new kind of book, the unfinished murder-mystery of *Edwin Drood*. But on June 8, 1870, he collapsed after a stroke and died the next day. He was buried in the Poets' Corner of Westminster Abbey on June 14. He was only fifty-eight. He had declared his preference for a quiet burial in the country but public opinion insisted on the supreme national tribute.

MR. CHARLES DICKENS'S TOUR, DURING THE AUTUMN OF 1858.

Town	Day	Date	Time
CLIFTON	Monday	Aug. 2	8 o'clock
EXETER	Tuesday	" 3	8
PLYMOUTH	Wednesday	" 4	8
"	Thursday	" 5	3 & 8
CLIFTON	Friday	" 6	8
WORCESTER	Tuesday	" 10	8
WOLVERHAMPTN	Wednesday	" 11	8
SHREWSBURY	Thursday	" 12	8
CHESTER	Friday	" 13	8
LIVERPOOL	Wednesday	" 18	8
"	Thursday	" 19	8
"	Friday	" 20	8
"	Saturday	" 21	3
DUBLIN	Monday	" 23	8
"	Tuesday	" 24	8
"	Wednesday	" 25	3 & 8
"	Thursday	" 26	8
BELFAST	Friday	" 27	8
"	Saturday	" 28	3 & 8
CORK	Monday	" 30	8
"	Tuesday	" 31	3 & 8
LIMERICK	Wednesday	Sept. 1	8
"	Thursday	" 2	8
HUDDERSFIELD	Wednesday	" 8	8
WAKEFIELD	Thursday	" 9	8
YORK	Friday	" 10	8
HARROWGATE	Saturday	" 11	3 & 8
SCARBOROUGH	Monday	" 13	3 & 8
HULL	Tuesday	" 14	8
LEEDS	Wednesday	" 15	8
HALIFAX	Thursday	" 16	8
SHEFFIELD	Friday	" 17	8
MANCHESTER	Saturday	" 18	8
DARLINGTON	Tuesday	" 21	8
DURHAM	Wednesday	" 22	8
SUNDERLAND	Thursday	" 23	8
NEWCASTLE	Friday	" 24	8
"	Saturday	" 25	3 & 8
EDINBURGH	Monday	" 27	8
"	Tuesday	" 28	8
"	Wednesday	" 29	3 & 8
"	Thursday	" 30	8
DUNDEE	Friday	Oct. 1	8
"	Saturday	" 2	8
ABERDEEN	Monday	" 4	3 & 8
PERTH	Tuesday	" 5	8
GLASGOW	Wednesday	" 6	8
"	Thursday	" 7	8
"	Friday	" 8	8
"	Saturday	" 9	3
BRADFORD	Thursday	" 14	8

Dickens's fondness for giving readings from his books led him to undertake country-wide tours, often performing at a different town each night. This itinerary shows the exhausting timetable he set himself for his autumn tour of 1858.

Dickens had written a vast amount, in spite of the pressure of a busy social life and public appearances. He was an exhausted man. His temperament was dynamic and mercurial with rapid alternations of mood. He quarrelled easily and quickly, but made many enduring and cordial friendships. His marriage was not a success. Kate, over-burdened with her numerous childbirths—they had ten children—was slow and gauche and could not keep pace with his career in society. He was devoted to two of her sisters; one, Mary, died young, a tragedy which he never forgot. The other, the practical Georgina, took over the management of his home and family. That was inevitably galling to Kate and the couple separated.

He had worn himself out at the desk and on the dais. He had risen from nothing to become a name renowned across the world, masterly in the comedy, the pathos and the portraiture of mankind in all its moods. If he was vain he had ample cause for self-satisfaction. He liked to call himself "The Inimitable" and that he had proved himself to be.

48 Doughty Street, now a Dickens Museum, where Charles and Kate spent the first two years of their married life.

Bleak House at Broadstairs in Kent, where Dickens spent many summers and did much of his writing.

Dickens, his wife Kate and her sister Mary, who lived with them until her sudden death in 1842. She was mourned by Dickens and is claimed to have been the inspiration for the character of "Little Nell" in The Old Curiosity Shop.

Two contemporary novelists. (Left) William Makepeace Thackeray (1811–63) whose reputation as a novelist rivalled that of Dickens. He was a social satirist, but only of the upper-class world he knew. Within this limited sphere he created characters of great depth, but he lacked Dickens's breadth of social vision. (Right) George Eliot (1819–80) whose novels of country and provincial life, particularly Middlemarch, have gained in appreciation since her death.

WHEN DICKENS suddenly emerged the field was open for a great popular story-teller. During his life the middle class rapidly multiplied in numbers and influence. Its members wanted books and could pay for them. They preferred very long books and were accustomed to read them in monthly instalments as they appeared in the magazines. The novelists of the previous century had often written in a lively and free-spoken way about the rogues and the raffish types; their public enjoyed bawdy elements in a tale of adventure. The new readers did not want such gay indecencies. They liked romantic and adventurous tales. Sir Walter Scott, who died four years before *The Pickwick Papers* began to appear, had written of the past, especially that of his own Scotland, ignoring the challenging theme of the industrialization that was transforming parts of Scotland.

In England there was more realism. Jane Austen had made delicate comedy of the middle-class families of the small squires and clergy who lived quietly in secluded comfort. But it was time for a larger survey of the nation's developing contrast of wealth and poverty. This evoked the great Victorian story-tellers who, while not dwelling on the more sordid aspects of life for the sake of sensationalism, gave a true picture of the social stress and struggles. Dickens, who had a wonderful eye for the humours, grievances, and follies of the men and women about him, set to work at the right moment. The market for his kind of story was waiting for him and he had capable rivals: William Makepeace Thackeray was a year older than Dickens but, outside journalism, he did not make his mark as a novelist until 1848 when *Vanity Fair* was published. Here was an author of stature but without the wide knowledge of the English people and the powerful comic force of Dickens. Marian Evans, who wrote as George Eliot, won a considerable public in the eighteen-fifties. Born in 1819, she had turned from scholarly journalism to fiction when she was forty and then in three years produced *Adam Bede, The Mill on the Floss,* and *Silas Marner*. Though an intellectual, she could write well of poor and earthy folk but she was not a competitor with Dickens for supremacy in the public favour. The Brontë sisters, fighting their way out of obscurity, derived their material from the North Country they knew, seen as rough and passionate in Emily's *Wuthering Heights*, more domesticated in the work of Charlotte and Anne, whose heroines were humble and virtuous young women.

Thackeray, at least in *Vanity Fair*, touched genius in characterization. But he lacked the continuing urgency and fertility of the supreme writers of fiction. Anthony Trollope (1815–82) had an immense output and his Barchester novels about the higher clergy which began with *The Warden* in 1855 have the masterly touch. Early in this century young people were told to read Thackeray to improve their English prose, and George Eliot because she was a "near-classic", and were rarely, if at all, recommended to Trollope. The revival of Trollope has been well justified. There is a rich social landscape in all his fiction, and not only in the scenes of cathedral and parochial life in which he excelled. In the case of Dickens the readers did not need any urging. He was compulsive because he campaigned for causes yet did it so very entertainingly. The phrase "as good as a play" was applicable to any of his books.

An unquenchable amateur actor, he loved any kind of professional Show Business.

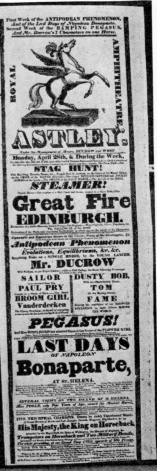

A poster advertising the diverse entertainments provided by Astley's Circus at the Royal Amphitheatre in Westminster.

Mr. GRIMALDI, as CLOWN

Joey Grimaldi performing in the pantomime of "Harlequin and Asmodeus" at the Theatre Royal, Covent Garden.

There was no intellectual theatre in his time. On the popular side he relished the "spectaculars" with equestrian feats at Astley's Amphitheatre in Westminster. He wrote sympathetically in *Hard Times* of circus clowns and acrobats whose times could indeed be hard as they grew stiff and jaded. He liked pantomimes. As a boy he was taken to see the famous clown Joseph Grimaldi (1779–1837) and later, in gratitude for the joy thus derived, he edited the memoirs of London's beloved "Joey". He nearly became a professional player himself, but fortunately for English literature he missed the chance of an audition at Covent Garden and lived by his pen.

He made glorious comedy of Vincent Crummles and his troupe in *Nicholas Nickleby*; they are caricatures of real figures on the road. These companies worked very hard for very little on circuits of small towns. One of their theatres in Yorkshire, at Richmond, has been perfectly preserved and can be visited. It is as beautiful in design and colour as it is small. Among its players as a lad, and later as a returning "star", was Edmund Kean who had a dynamic, demonic impetus in Shakespearian roles. He ruined his career by dissipation whereas William Charles Macready (1793–1873), described by Tennyson as "grave, moral, and sublime", raised the status of his profession and the whole standard of theatrical production. He became a friend of Dickens. One of his achievements was to rescue Shakespeare from absurdly re-written texts. A similar service was rendered by Edmund Phelps, who became actor-manager at Sadler's Wells in North London in 1844 and stayed for twenty years.

Robert Browning (1812–89) and Elizabeth Barrett Browning (1806–61). The romance of their relationship tends to be remembered more often than their quality as poets.

Matthew Arnold (1822–88), the son of a famous headmaster of Rugby School, combined writing poetry and literary criticism with being an inspector of schools. His personal campaign was against the commonplace and utilitarian in life and art.

Rising out of the Crummles' world with its tribulations on tour came the Terry family, which contributed a long line of talents to the Victorian stage. The particular glory of the family was Ellen Terry who appeared as a child actress with Kean's son Charles in 1856 when she was nine. She later became the leading lady with Sir Henry Irving at the Lyceum Theatre. There was still a strong Puritan belief that the theatre was a wicked place. The great Victorian actors overcame this and made play-going acceptable to even the strictest families.

Then the play mattered less than the players who were judged by their performance in traditional and especially Shakespearian roles. Macready bravely tried to introduce poets of the day and produced with little success two plays by Robert Browning (1812–89), a rising literary talent whose work in the theatre proved ineffective. Browning was born in Camberwell in the same year as Dickens. His father, a clerk in the Bank of England, did not force him to earn a commercial living and with this freedom and leisure he climbed gradually to eminence along with his wife Elizabeth Barrett (1806–61), whose poetry had charmed him before he met her and was acclaimed before his own. He rescued her from the invalid's bedroom in which she had been secluded.

Alfred Tennyson, three years Browning's senior, became Poet Laureate, succeeding Wordsworth, in 1850, the year in which his *In Memoriam* appeared. Before that moving

Queen Victoria and Prince Albert at Windsor, painted by Sir Edwin Landseer in the early 1840s.

A chair made of japanned papier mâché in the extravagant style which characterized so many of the objects shown in the Great Exhibition of 1862. Though rather remote from furniture in daily use, this was the sort of item that influenced Victorian taste in interior decoration.

and melodious lament for his friend, Henry Hallam, he had not been fully appreciated but now he could do no wrong. He was able to mix poetry, not mere versification, with patriotism. Browning could be obscure and baffling. Tennyson was lucid. It was said that his command of language was more impressive than his powers of thought. But he soothed Victorian doubts with his blend of vague theology, piety, and romantic liberalism, trusting that "somehow good will be the final goal of ill". This optimistic and complacent view of society was not shared by Dickens who was not asked to read his works to Queen Victoria, as Tennyson had been, and who was at last received by her only in the year of his death.

Nor was it the outlook of Algernon Swinburne (1837–1909), dissipated and rebellious in his youth and the idol of the radically-minded young. His fluent rhythms and torrent of word-music were accompanied by a far from conventional view of morality. In 1866 the sensuality of his *Poems and Ballads* shocked the public who in 1859 had been delighted by the orthodox morality as well as by the suave cadences of Tennyson's *Idylls of the King*.

That the prosperous Victorians were insensitive to beauty was a growing accusation. The name Philistine was given to the enemies of the arts by Matthew Arnold (1822–88), a Professor of Poetry at Oxford who was also a fine poet with a Tennysonian richness. He asked for "sweetness and light" as a contrast to the darkness of a society whose barbarism he denounced. John Ruskin (1819–1900), who began to write and lecture on

14

painting and architecture in the eighteen-fifties, shared Arnold's disgust with Victorian materialism. Ruskin carried the attack from the arts to the field of commercial morality. George Bernard Shaw (1856–1950) later hailed him as a Socialist, but Ruskin's primary concern was with the ugliness of Victorian capitalism.

If there had been a Painter Laureate as well as a Poet Laureate, Sir Edwin Landseer (1802–73) would certainly have held that position. He was an Englishman and Franz Winterhalter, the favourite portrait-painter of the Royal Family, was not. Landseer was a superb draughtsman but his painting of mountain scenery, deer, and dogs had a lush and sentimental facility which was much derided after his death. Queen Victoria loved his work and his admiration of the Scottish Highlands. He was a guest at Balmoral and tutor in art to the Queen. He suited the romanticism of the period as much as did the music of the German composer, Felix Mendelssohn (1809–47), who frequently visited England. Much to the taste of the time were the airs and operas of Michael Balfe (1808–70), an Irishman whose *Bohemian Girl*, produced in 1843, was a principal favourite of the public. It was not a fruitful epoch for British music.

A revolt against the trend in pictorial art was led by Sir John Everett Millais (1829–96), a founder of the Pre-Raphaelite school with Holman Hunt and Dante Gabriel Rossetti (1828–82), the poet-painter. He broke with "the grand style" and worked for simplicity and sincerity. The revolt against complacent materialism took several forms. There was a discovery of and a new interest in the beauty achieved by the builders and

15

A view of Lower Manhattan, New York, from Brooklyn Heights in 1849, just after the date of Dickens's first visit to America.

craftsmen of the Middle Ages. One aspect of this was the Gothic revival in architecture, but the movement influenced many other fields of design and art. The immensely versatile William Morris (1834–96) was influential as a poet, a designer of furniture and wall-papers, and as a printer. He thought that the appearance of a book could be as valuable as its contents. He was a medievalist who found his models in the past and used them in all his crafts to decorate and enrich the present. Like the Pre-Raphaelite painters he was very influential in spreading the taste for old forms. Rich people wishing to be thought cultured favoured the interior decoration in which Morris excelled. The fault of the movement was to encourage antiquarian styles where they were out of place. For country houses the serene Georgian style was abandoned for huge and inconvenient homes with towers and spires. Queen Victoria's Balmoral, her holiday home in Scotland, planned by herself and her husband, set a fashion in the eighteen-fifties for imitation fortresses. A striking example of Gothic out-of-place was the construction of the new Law Courts in London. Many educational and civic buildings were erected as though the date was 1450, not 1850. But Dickens was not much concerned with this aspect of change. He was more excited by the strangeness of human character than by the vagaries of the artists.

During his two American visits Dickens established a warm friendship with leading American authors in New York and New England. He had their support in his campaign against the piratical American publishers who exploited the absence of copyright in English books, printed his novels without permission and paid him nothing. He was delighted to meet Washington Irving (1783–1859), who had worked as a diplomat in the American Embassy in London and showed a happy knowledge of English life in his *Sketch-Books*. Of Irving, Dickens wrote that there was no author living whose approbation he would be more proud to earn and that the *Sketch-Books* were his regular bed-books. Edgar Allan Poe (1809–49) wanted Dickens to find him London publishers and, as this proved to be difficult, there was some coolness between them. But with Henry Wadsworth Longfellow (1807–82), whom he entertained in London and later at Gad's Hill, he had a close and abiding comradeship. During his second journey in 1867–68, though puzzled by the Transcendental philosophy of Ralph Waldo Emerson (1803–82), he had cordial meetings with him. Oliver Wendell Holmes (1809–94) was another whom he met with pleasure and affection. On the whole Dickens seemed to get on better with some American than with English authors. It is true that they were not, like Thackeray, his immediate competitors for renown, but his friendships in New England were genuine as well as warm.

The Houses of Parliament, built 1840–60, were the first public buildings to be designed in the newly-revived Gothic style. Charles Barry, an architect of the classic school, provided the basic plan while Augustus Pugin, a medievalist, detailed the building in all its Gothic ornaments.

THE ELECTIONS of the eighteenth century had been farcical. Towns which had declined over the centuries and which had only a handful of voters still retained a Member of Parliament and were really the political property of the big land-owners, while some of the large new manufacturing towns were hardly represented at all. This state of affairs was partially ended by the Reform Act of 1832 which was passed by Parliament amid outbreaks of violence and threats of more to come. The constituencies represented in the House of Commons were reduced by more than a quarter, but the right to vote was not widely extended. Only those with houses whose annual rental was £10 were given this right, and there were few urban workers and no country labourers in that class. Dickens, who reported the debates, was not impressed by this paltry concession to popular government. Nor were the Radicals, now a growing force, who wanted far more reform.

Some of the extremists were known as Chartists. There were six demands in their Charter for democracy, the most important of which was for votes for all men. Nothing was said of women's rights. For a while during the eighteen-forties Chartist clamour frightened the ordinary citizens since some of its campaigners were advocating the use of force. When a great meeting on Kennington Common was announced there was much apprehension of riot and even revolution. Londoners barricaded homes and offices, and the troops were called out. Then the Chartist extremists found most of their supporters unready for drastic action. The great meeting was a failure and Chartism faded out by 1850.

Dickens himself, though his politics were Radical, had a horror of political violence. Particularly vivid evidence of that is his lurid description in *The Old Curiosity Shop* of a popular upheaval in the Midlands. He wrote of "maddened men, armed with sword and fire-brand, rushing forth, despite the protests of their wives, on errands of destruction to work no ruin so surely as their own". Such hideous chaos never came, but Dickens remained haunted by a vision of mob rule. He liked the poor as individuals but distrusted them in the mass.

Dickens was asked to stand for Parliament and refused. He had seen enough of Parliamentary procedure from the reporters' gallery and wisely decided that he had better things to do. As a reformer he could expose abuses with the unique power of his pen. There was plenty to attack. The conditions in the mines, mills, and factories remained appalling by the standards of today. Dickens could fairly claim that the Doodles of one party, as he called them, were the Foodles of the other. There were only two Parties, apart from the Irish Nationalists demanding Home Rule for their country and not getting it until the next century. The Whigs or Liberals represented the new industrial and urban capitalists, while the Tories championed the landowners. The mass of the workers had only their labour to sell and since there was no scarcity of labour they could not get a fair wage. The poor man had to take what wage he could get, having little to hope for from either party. He had not yet thought of organizing his own political party and Trade Unions were only just beginning to be formed effectively in the eighteen-fifties. There was no Labour Party until 1900 when two Labour Members of Parliament were elected.

The growth of the coal and iron industries in the late eighteenth and early nineteenth century in England made possible the application of steam power, the development

Children at work in a textile mill in the 1840s.

of machinery, and the consequent adoption of the factory system. This brought about the change from a mainly agricultural economy to an industrial one and is known as the Industrial Revolution. At the same time the population had been increasing greatly, so there were swarms of poor people ready to man the machines: they were totally unorganized and the employers were rapacious. The exploitation of women and children in the mines, mills, and factories had been scandalous. In 1819 a Cotton Mills Act limited the hours in which children might be employed to seventy-two a week. Even this reform was not properly enforced since supervision was left, not to Government inspectors, but to magistrates who might be careless or corrupt.

The working conditions for children in the coal mines were even worse than in the mills. Boys and girls too were sent down them at the age of five. Not till 1842 did Parliament prohibit all female labour underground and limit the recruitment of lads working in the pits. It now seems incredible that the age fixed for permissible boy-labour in the mines was ten. A Commission of Inquiry had reported in 1842 that the children had been "chained, belted, and harnessed like dogs" to pull the trucks of coal.

Another form of child-slavery was the apprenticing of workhouse children to master chimney-sweeps at the age of six or seven, a fate narrowly escaped by Oliver Twist. Being so small these little wretches could squirm their way up narrow chimneys. Often they were terrified and were then forced on by the lighting of a fire underneath them. Measures were passed in 1840 and 1864 intended to make this kind of apprenticeship illegal, but there was much evasion and the abominable system was not completely stopped until 1874.

Women and children at work in the mines were expected to drag tubs of coal by means of a belt and chain around the waist.

A great reformer was the Earl of Shaftesbury (1801–85). He entered the House of Commons at the age of twenty-five and succeeded to an earldom in 1851. It was largely due to him that Parliament accepted a Ten Hours Act which restricted hours of adult as well as child labour. This was opposed by some Liberals who believed that their Free-Trade doctrines (that no country should restrict trade by imposing import duty) should extend to unrestricted use of labour with no State interference. Lord Shaftesbury's broader view prevailed with difficulty. He also championed education of poor children from the city slums by opening special schools financed by charity, and the better housing of the poor through the Lodging House Act of 1851, which was described by Dickens as "the best piece of legislation that ever issued from Parliament".

The national conscience about the "sweated labour" of women and children had been quickened by authors as well as reformers. Especially effective had been Thomas Hood's *Song of the Shirt*, a condemnation of conditions in the clothing trade, where women had to work incredibly long hours to earn a very small wage, and Elizabeth Barrett Browning's *The Cry of the Children*, written in 1844, which contained the lines:

> For all day long we drag our burden tiring
> Through the coal-dark underground
> Or all the day we drive the wheels of iron
> In the factories, round and round.

It was not great poetry, but it helped to give the complacent public a necessary shock. But "sweated labour" remained, especially for the sempstress, until 1914 when economic conditions changed during the First World War. A period of full employment caused by the war enabled the women to win a fairer return for their labour.

A natural reaction now to the horrors of Victorian industrialization is to ask what the Trade Unions were doing about this. The answer is simple. They either did not exist or were too weak to do anything in the first half of the century. In 1800

Low travelling in a coal mine in 1878. Men were expected to move about and to cut coal in tunnels as narrow as this, as well as cope with all the attendant hazards of working underground —the risk of explosions, flooding and rock falls.

A Hiring Fair at Spitalfields in 1850 where, on Mondays and Tuesdays, young children hired themselves out for work for the ensuing week. Girls of nine and ten undertook to clean, wash, rinse and cook for families who were at work and required temporary servants. The wages ranged from one shilling to one and fourpence a week.

"combination" of labourers had been made illegal. The French Revolution had terrified the property-owning class in Britain who feared that any organization of the workers would lead to bloodshed and robbery. The Combination Acts which made Trade Unions illegal were repealed in 1824, but there was still repression. In 1834 some farm-labourers in a Dorset village called Tolpuddle were convicted of conspiracy in restraint of trade and transported to Australia as criminals. But opinion was slowly changing and they were pardoned and brought home in 1836. They were long remembered as the Tolpuddle Martyrs.

But still the workers had little or no protection and were afraid of organizing for defence. A leading social reformer, Robert Owen, launched an ambitious scheme for a Grand Consolidated Trade Union in 1833 and there was a National Miners Association started in 1841, but both collapsed. A Union which was to survive and to become one of the largest and most powerful was the Amalgamated Society of Engineers founded in 1851. In *Hard Times* Dickens revealed both his loathing of the hard-hearted employers, typified by Bounderby and Gradgrind, and his dislike of Trade Union agitators, typified by Slackbridge in the story. Once more his sympathy was for the working

23

Caged prisoners on a transportation ship bound for Botany Bay, Australia.

people as individuals, but he saw the danger of a tyrannical majority intolerant of any individual who held his own views and went his own way.

Female labour was abominably exploited in factories, mills, and workshops. This encouraged women to go into domestic service, of course at wages which now seem unbelievably low. For educated women there was little employment except as poorly paid teachers in schools and as governesses in the prosperous homes. The Brontë sisters, before they took to authorship, had had a bitter taste of both these careers. Charlotte, for example, was twice a governess in the late eighteen-thirties, and her salary at one post was twenty pounds a year, out of which she had to find her clothes and pocket-money. A governess had a humiliating life, half-way between the drawing-room and the Servants' Hall. For middle-class girls there were no careers in the professions or as secretaries in business offices. When they married, those women who had any property could not claim and use it as their own. The Married Women's Property Act, establishing feminine rights

24

BE UNITED AND INDUSTRIOUS

AMALGAMATED SOCIETY OF ENGINEERS, MACHINISTS, MILLWRIGHTS, SMITHS, AND PATTERN MAKERS.

This is to Certify that   was admitted a Member of the Branch on the   day of   18 In witness whereof we have subscribed our names and affixed the Society's Seal.

PRESIDENT   SECRETARY

A Trade Union card for the Amalgamated Society of Engineers, Machinists, Millwrights, Smiths and Pattern Makers, which survives today as one of the strongest Trade Unions.

ROYAL GARDENS
VAUXHALL,
PRICES OF REFRESHMENTS.

	s.	d.		s.	d.
A Chicken	4	0	Sparkling Moselle	8	6
Dish of Ham	1	0	Madeira	7	0
Broiled ditto	1	6	Claret	6	0
Sandwich	1	0	Old Hock, Iced	10	0
Half ditto	0	6	Champagne, Moett's	12	0
Quarter Ditto	0	3	Pints	6	0
Dish of Tongue	1	0	Champagne	10	0
Dish of Beef	1	0	Pints, ditto	5	6
Plate of Collared Beef	1	0	Arrack, per bowl	10	0
Plate of Collared Veal	1	0	Ditto ditto, small size	5	0
Pigeon Pie	3	6	Ditto ditto, smallest size	2	6
Rump Steak Pie	2	6	Ditto ditto, per glass	1	6
Veal and Ham Pie	2	6	Gin and Water	0	6
Lobsters	2	6	Rum and Water	0	6
Tart	1	0	Whiskey and Water	0	6
Cheesecake	0	2	Brandy and Water	1	0
Heartcake	0	2	Guinness's Stout, per bottle	1	0
Shrewsbury Cake	0	2	Small ditto	0	6
Biscuit	0	1	Sparkling Edinburgh Ale,		
Salad, including ingredients	1	0	per bottle	1	0
Plate of Cheese	0	3	Small ditto	0	6
Pat of Butter	0	2	Bass's Pale Ale, per bottle	1	0
Slice of Bread	0	1	Small ditto	0	6
Small Rack of Bread	0	6	Stout, per jug	0	8
Plate of Pastry	1	0	Small ditto	0	6
Coffee or Tea, per cup	0	6	Soda Water, Carrara		
Port	5	0	Water, and Lemonade	0	6
Fine Old ditto	6	0	Ginger Beer	0	4
Pints, ditto	3	0	Ices, per glass	1	0
Sherry	5	0	Ditto	0	6
Fine Old ditto	6	0	Sherry Cobbler	1	0
Pints, ditto	3	0	Cigars	0	3
Bucellas	5	0			

George Cruikshank

London Recreations

(Left) The Royal Gardens at Vauxhall was one of the grandiose pleasure gardens of the time, where the rich could go to enjoy firework displays, concerts and entertainments of all kinds. Food was much cheaper in the shops of the poor districts.

(Right) One of George Cruikshank's illustrations for Sketches by Boz *in which Dickens's clerks and their families are enjoying a day out at a rural tea-garden.*

in ownership, was not passed until 1882. The Dickensian world was a man's world.

It was not, as he depicted it, altogether a miserable world. If wages were low so were prices. Some of today's luxuries were available to all. Mr. Pickwick's man-servant, Sam Weller, remarked that "Poverty and oysters always seem to go together". Drinking spirits provided a cheap escape. Dickens ridiculed teetotallers, but he denounced the gin-palaces in which the poorest could forget their grievances for a few pence. He also raged against the strictness of Sunday Observance; on the day of rest there were no public recreations. Only the public houses were open. Yet in the *Sketches by Boz* there are many pictures of the underpaid clerks having a gay time quite cheaply on the river and in pleasure-gardens. A few pence went a very long way. Dickens never concealed in his novels the misery caused by penury. But there is a constant reminder that the most deprived did not lose their sense of humour. Even in the worst conditions his characters could sometimes jest and revel.

WHEN A census was taken in 1811, the year before the birth of Charles Dickens, the population of the United Kingdom was just under thirteen and a quarter millions. In 1871, a year after his death, it was nearly twenty-seven and a half million. As the numbers rose the general way of life, especially in methods of travel, was completely altered. When Dickens first went to work news and letters, as well as passengers, made the journeys at the speed of a horse. In 1840 teams of four carried the Royal Mail from London to Glasgow. In a rapidly driven coach, with changes of horses quickly made, a rate of ten miles an hour could be expected. Thus a man who lived in Brighton and had business in London fifty-two miles away could, with an early start, go there and back in a day and have some hours in the capital.

But the ten hours spent on the road covering the hundred and four miles that this journey involved were accompanied by hazards. There were coaches which turned over. In one of the *Sketches by Boz* the members of a family planning a trip to Ramsgate prefer to go by sea because they think the coaches are too dangerous. The perils of road transport did not begin with the motor car. There was the discomfort as well as the danger of ten hours' driving. Yet Dickens never lost his affection for horse and carriage and, when he was prosperously settled at his last home near Rochester, he would take his guests for a drive in an old coach with red-jacketed postillions and a horn blowing. He also enjoyed a trip on the river. He never accepted the newly introduced railways gladly. He accused them of adding to the smoke and dirt in the towns and of polluting the countryside. His affection for the coach and horses and the warm welcome at the

27

roadside inns did not diminish, and long after the railways had spread across the country he was dating his books back and describing coaching days.

Steam powered transport had first come into use on the water. A pioneer was Henry Bell's *Comet* which made regular voyages from Glasgow to Greenock on the Clyde in 1812. The Thames had its steamers in 1814, and in the eighteen-thirties Dickens described the Londoners who liked to have summer villas down the estuary and went to and from their work daily by water with ample refreshments served on board. But the railways were beginning to compete. The first London terminus was London Bridge, into which the London and Greenwich line began to run in 1836. Then railway development was rapid and general. Euston was opened for the London to Birmingham line just after the accession of Queen Victoria in the summer of 1837. That line had forced its way through the north-west of London where Dickens lived as a boy. In *Dombey and Son* he had much to say of the upheaval that it caused. Housing, most of it wretched, replaced the old market-gardens with greenhouses and peaches and the waste-land with snipe on the wing. The engine-driver replaced the man who held the reins.

People were infected with a kind of railway madness during the eighteen-forties. Anything labelled "railway" would sell. Dickens described how the old inn became the Railway Arms and the Ham and Beef Shop the Railway Eating House. The development of the lines was rapid and profitable. Capitalists, typified by George Hudson, "the Railway King", made fortunes and did not always keep them. There was a slump in the over-valued shares in 1848 and Hudson ended in ruin. There were no bulldozers to speed the labour of cutting tracks and laying the rails. The navvies, so named because they had previously made the navigations as the canals were called, were turned on to the new need. With hand-labour cheap and plentiful their spade-work soon made the profitable tracks. Some landowners resisted the intrusion on their estates, but they came to see the advantages of surrender to the inevitable. There were no planning authorities to question and delay innovations. It has been accurately called the Age of Anyhow and some of the results were disastrous as the new industrial developments went ahead.

There were keen minds and great abilities at work as well as unscrupulous financiers

THE GREAT WESTERN.

Passing Portishead Point on her first Voyage to New York.

To the Directors & Proprietors of the Great Western Steamship Company, have, with the aid of their talented Engineer, M.r Brunel, triumphantly succeeded in...

of whom Dickens wrote fiercely, especially in *Little Dorrit*, of which Bernard Shaw said that it contained more revolutionary material than the works of Karl Marx. A remarkable example of brilliant versatility was Isambard Kingdom Brunel (1806–59). From 1833 to 1846 he was the chief engineer of the Great Western Railway and within a comparatively short life he combined remarkable achievements as railway-line draughtsman, bridge-builder, and ship-designer. The first steam-ship to cross the Atlantic regularly was his vessel called *Great Western* which crossed from Bristol to New York in sixteen days in 1838. When Dickens made his first journey to America in January 1842 he and his wife travelled in *Britannia*, a vessel of only 1,154 tons. It had one tall funnel,

A lithograph of Brunel's "Great Western" passing Portishead Point on her first voyage to New York.

29

Isambard Kingdom Brunel (1806–59)—a great and versatile engineer. As well as his achievements in the fields of marine and railway engineering, he designed a complete prefabricated hospital building which was shipped in parts to the Crimea in 1855.

(Below) King's Cross station just after it was completed, looking very much as it does today.

large paddles, and three masts for sails. It was a bad month to choose, the weather was stormy, and the sufferings of the emigrant steerage passengers, vividly described in *Martin Chuzzlewit*, were appalling. But they got there safely in a ship which would now be thought small for a Channel crossing.

The railways to and from the north came to the verge of Early Victorian London, but were not allowed to penetrate into the Duke of Bedford's well-planned Bloomsbury estate, so the great stations were sited in a row along the Euston Road. They were ambitiously built. Euston had its huge Grecian arch designed by Philip Hardwick which, to the regret of many, was removed as an encumbrance a century and a quarter later. King's Cross still has a fine frontage by Lewis Cubitt. For the last of the three, St. Pancras, Sir George Gilbert Scott followed the new taste for Gothic in 1868. Its soaring spires still have their admirers owing to a revived vogue for Victorian styles in decoration.

By that time London had its Underground Railway linking Paddington with Farringdon Street. The tunnelling had been difficult and dangerous. The line was opened in 1863 when Mr. Gladstone, then Chancellor of the Exchequer, was carried along it with a party of notables in an open truck. The public were soon to be better accommodated, but the steam-engines belched smoke and for a long time the Underground was no place for clean linen. The Londoners of the time were accustomed to fog, fumes and filthy streets. Nobody would claim that the huge, built-up and over-crowded area of today has the attraction of a city of limited size; but at least it has washed its face to some extent.

Mr. Gladstone and a party of notables making the first journey on the Paddington to Farringdon Street underground railway in an open truck.

For urban transport the omnibus had been put on the streets by a Mr. Shillibeer in 1829. They were large vehicles drawn by three horses harnessed side by side. The conductors known as "cads" had all sorts of tricks for inveigling extra passengers for whom there were no seats vacant and for whom the journey was most uncomfortable. But they could not escape until they paid their fare of sixpence, quite a lot at that time. As Boz put it, quoting one of the "cads", these victims were properly "done over" until they "forked out the stumpy".

The rich had their own carriages or coaches; public transport was available in hackney cabs whose average speed in town was six miles an hour. Some were rickety and collapsed. When Mr. Pickwick was "cabbin' it" Sam Weller described him as "having two miles of danger at eightpence". The tall and good-looking two-seater cab with a driver at the back of the roof was introduced in 1834 and took the name of its inventor, John Aloysius Hansom. The hansoms survived until the beginning of this century. They moved far more quickly than the four-wheeled hackney cabs and were better suited to those in a hurry or wanting to cut a dash. The drivers up aloft were lively characters and always ready with a quip or a taunt to the slower vehicles.

(Above) "Boneshaker" bicycles of this type, manufactured in France, became very popular in England in the late 1860s, and cycle racing was the new sport.

A private hansom cab of the late nineteenth century. These one-horse carriages were particularly stable and easy to manœuvre, and therefore became a popular form of transport.

DICKENS FOUNDED a magazine and was in charge of it for twenty years. He chose *Household Words* as its title. This name, now seeming rather hum-drum, declared the nature of the public which he sought and won. While it contained plenty of fiction, including some of his best, it also made demands for various reforms. One of the early features was a series of *Happy Family* articles.

Dickens affirmed his belief in the domestic virtues. He valued and commended home life because it was intimate and personal. He delighted in Christmas reunions at the fireside and his Christmas Stories have remained great favourites. What he hated was the remote control of people's behaviour and destinies by Government offices and the arbitrary rule of Boards and Corporations. The amount of interference suffered by people today would have enraged him. Resenting vast accumulations by plutocrats of property in stocks and shares, he believed that the poor man's property with a roof, four walls, a fire in the hearth and modest furnishing was the staple of his independence. This kind of home was for him the essential element of English life.

The mansions of the rich, pompously furnished and lavishly staffed, he described with contempt for their wastefulness and lack of taste. It has been estimated that in Victorian England as much as a sixth of the population were engaged in personal service, including the haughty men-servants in their "yellow plush" uniforms, who were also ridiculed by Thackeray, the dozens of maids housed in the attics and basements, and the coachmen and grooms in the stables.

The main rooms were large and were filled with massive furniture. Mahogany was in vogue. At the sale of Mr. Dombey's house and furniture the workmen appear "upheaving perfect rocks of Spanish mahogany, best rosewood and plate glass". In Mr. Podsnap's house near Portman Square everything had to be big, including the mirrors and the table silver. "Hideous solidity was the characteristic of the Podsnap plate. Everything was made to look as heavy as it could and take up as much room as possible." Dickens was not afraid of exaggeration. He stressed the size and overlooked the possible elegance of the candelabra and huge chandeliers. All rich Victorians were not vulgarians.

33

(*Above*) *A beautiful Minton porcelain vase in the sort of design that was much copied for popular use and which we now think of as being typically "Victorian".*

A "flower" arrangement of shells, enclosed in a glass case. Such bulky monstrosities enjoyed an incomprehensible popularity.

Recently the quality as well as the quantity of their chattels has been acknowledged.

Upholstery was sumptuous. No surface and no mantelpiece was to be left bare. Vases and bric-à-brac were everywhere. A glass case containing wax fruit was a frequent decoration. When, with the invention of photography, personal portraits became generally available they were framed in silver and displayed in the sitting-rooms. The walls, being vast, needed the huge paintings of the type shown at the Royal Academy's Summer Exhibition. To furnish a room was to smother it in evidence of opulence. But there was a point in this over-loading. There was no central heating and a coal-fire on one side of a large room, with most of the heat going up the chimney, leaves a chilly vacuum in winter. To fill the vacuum with abundance of furniture and to curtain the windows generously mitigated the cold.

The tall, narrow, Victorian London home of a prosperous family with five or six unheated stories and no lifts was designed for a class which was sure of unfailing supplies of cheap domestic labour. The Mayfair part of the West End of London had mostly been developed before Dickens was born. During his time the big development came north of Hyde Park, long known as Tyburnia after the old site for public hangings, and later as Bayswater. In *Our Mutual Friend* the "bran-new" Mr. and Mrs. Veneering with all their furniture new had a new house in a new fashionable quarter, typical of Bayswater's Lancaster Gate, then a haunt of the rich parvenu. The huge houses were going up here during the eighteen-fifties. In this area John Galsworthy (1867–1933), the novelist and playwright, settled his Forsytes who believed that an Englishman's home was not only his castle but a fortress to be well barricaded with the mahogany furniture favoured by the Dickensian magnates.

The small homes were spreading in all directions, sometimes in gracious suburbs and sometimes in squalid disarray. Veneering's clerk, Reginald Wilfer, lived in Holloway. Close to his humble household was "a tract of suburban Sahara, where tiles and bricks were burned, bones were boiled, carpets beaten, and rubbish shot!" There were also repulsive mounds of mingled ordure and litter, the property of contractors who sifted through them for anything of value. Yet such homes had their happiness. Contemplating his surroundings Mr. Wilfer said, "What might have been is not what is," and "made the best of his way to the end of his journey". The patience of the poor householder was often described by Dickens. In all directions the two-storey houses of the pound-a-week wage-earner (Scrooge paid Bob Cratchit less than a pound) were being run up. Dickens did not see their occupants as necessarily miserable. They often had space for a lodger which helped with the cost of living. There was no room and no money for mahogany, plate glass, and wax-fruit but there would be a wealth of humbler ornaments.

Dickens never sentimentalized extreme poverty. He exposed the scandal of the slum houses in the great "rookeries", as he called the decaying piles of tenements in the

George Cruikshank

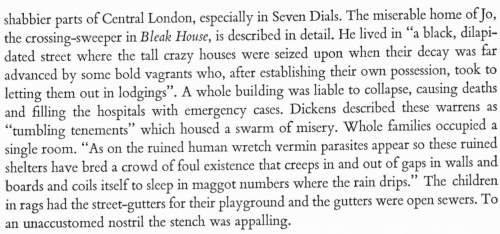

Monmouth Street, where second-hand clothes were bought and sold and the children played, as elsewhere, in the filthy street gutters.

(Below) A poke bonnet of white silk. This style was particularly popular in the 1830s.

shabbier parts of Central London, especially in Seven Dials. The miserable home of Jo, the crossing-sweeper in *Bleak House*, is described in detail. He lived in "a black, dilapidated street where the tall crazy houses were seized upon when their decay was far advanced by some bold vagrants who, after establishing their own possession, took to letting them out in lodgings". A whole building was liable to collapse, causing deaths and filling the hospitals with emergency cases. Dickens described these warrens as "tumbling tenements" which housed a swarm of misery. Whole families occupied a single room. "As on the ruined human wretch vermin parasites appear so these ruined shelters have bred a crowd of foul existence that creeps in and out of gaps in walls and boards and coils itself to sleep in maggot numbers where the rain drips." The children in rags had the street-gutters for their playground and the gutters were open sewers. To an unaccustomed nostril the stench was appalling.

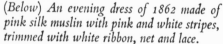

The inhabitants of such a district could only buy the cheapest garments or old clothes discarded by the prosperous and given to their servants who sold them. Dickens said that in one section of this area, called Monmouth Street, there was "the only true and real emporium for second-hand wearing apparel". There were vast stocks of boots and shoes among which people rummaged for something within their means. Here was a veritable Rag Fair for those who had to replace their old tatters with another set of garments, also tattered. Some of the stuff for sale had once been the finery of wealthier folk, and so the needy men and women who wanted some display could find a bit of colour and parade after work at the street-corners sporting these sorry relics of splendour.

Areas of this kind were often scenes of drunken violence. They were also a breeding-ground of crime. Here scoundrels like Fagin taught their young recruits how to steal and conducted a secret trade in the watches and wallets that had been snatched by the Artful Dodgers. Bad housing often encourages the worst kind of behaviour and the police, though

strengthened and reinforced while Dickens was a young man, had a strenuous life in coping with the brawlers and the robbers.

What was hanging in the huge wardrobes of the great houses? Since fashions change so rapidly it is impossible to follow them all through the life of Dickens. He was born in Jane Austen's England with its silken elegance for the men who could afford it. He died amid the broad-cloth solemnity of the mid-Victorians. If we select his middle period, 1840 to 1850, the picture is of dandies (and Dickens was quite a fop himself) wearing coloured frock-coats, almost femininely waisted, over narrow trousers strapped under their boots. To wear "low shoes" was a sign of poverty in men. A blue coat with shining brass buttons, a Georgian relic, was still favoured, but the vogue for black was beginning to prevail among business and professional men. This trend was stimulated by the mourning for the death of the Prince Consort in 1862. Top-hats grew taller and taller. The neck was hidden by a large cravat elaborately swathed round a high linen collar. In the illustrations to Dickens's first book Mr. Pickwick still wears the Georgian "tights" above top boots, but this only serves to mark him as an old-fashioned gentleman. Trousers had become universal, and tight-laced or elastic-sided boots, highly polished, had replaced the long Hessians and Wellingtons. The man who wanted to cut a dash showed his taste in a gay waistcoat.

At the same time the women were laden with clothing. James Laver, a specialist in the history of costume, wrote of the trends in 1840, "If women have never dressed so scantily as they did in 1800 they have probably never been so warmly clad as in the forties. Five or six petticoats, with much solid padding, were quite normal." The introduction in 1852 of the crinoline, a cage of cane or metal to support a lady's skirt without an excessive number of petticoats, gave women greater liberty of movement. Hats varied from the poke bonnet to the large straw trimmed with lace or flowers. Gay shawls and scarves were fashionable. A small waist was essential and was made to appear even smaller by the contrast of flowing sleeves above and the great hoop of the crinoline below. Men's fashions changed little. The top-hat soared above an increasing sprout of side-whiskers, and the fops had discovered the attraction of check trousers worn below a brown frock-coat and a gaily coloured waistcoat.

The Victorians were great wrappers-up. Their under-heated houses demanded indoor wear that we should use out-of-doors and in winter. When Major Joey Bagstock went by train with Mr. Dombey to Leamington in summer he took with him not a raincoat but "a pile of cloaks and great-coats". In the coaching years a long session on the roof in all weathers would have been intolerable without a capacious "surtout" and plenty of heavy cloth underneath it. Thrift demanded that garments should last. The wealthy "dossy" folk, who got that slang adjective from Count D'Orsay, a noted Victorian beau, might change their wardrobe according to the trend, but the middle class wanted value for money and preferred substantial fabrics.

It is noticeable in a photograph of Dickens reading to his daughters in the garden of Gad's Hill, obviously in summer, that he is wearing a heavy, tweedy-looking suit, and a thick waistcoat. The girls seem not to be so heavily clad but they are completely covered from neck to ankle. It was not an age of stripping and sun-worship. The sun was something to be evaded by drawing curtains or carrying a parasol. The women, if they bathed at the seaside, were voluminously concealed. The only exposure permissible was in the ball-room where necks and shoulders could be bare. The dancers were generating their own heat below the glittering chandeliers.

A pair of shoes worn by Queen Victoria at her coronation.

THE BOYS' schools described most vividly by Dickens in his novels are at worst abominable beyond words or, at their least bad, incompetent. Yet he himself in the two schools which he attended, first in Chatham and then in London, was not victimized. He had a kindly and competent master at the former, one who realized and stimulated the exceptional talent of his pupil. Of the latter he recorded his memories in an article in *Household Words* which is preserved in the volume of *Reprinted Pieces*. He thought very poorly of the headmaster but was kind about the over-worked usher and said that the Latin master was an excellent scholar and took pains when he saw "intelligence and a desire to learn"; those qualities were easily discernible in the young Master Dickens.

David Copperfield reveals much of the author's own life, but the boys' misery at Salem House, kept by the ignorant bully Mr. Creakle, is an invention. Young Charles never went to a boarding school. The macabre pictures of the odious Creakle and his pitiful assistant Mr. Mell cannot have been based on any academy attended by the author. But that does not prove them to be false in general. He had been to the high, bleak moors of North Yorkshire made infamous by schools where illegitimate and unwanted boys were sent to be kept out of their parents' way. That he found quite such a heartless and sadistic bully as Squeers, the headmaster of Dotheboys Hall in *Nicholas*

A village Dame School in the 1850s, where children of all ages were kept out of mischief during the day and managed somehow to learn the rudiments of reading.

39

Nickleby, is unlikely. The novelist frequently exaggerated to score a point. The savagely brutal Squeers made a good story and there were schools in the county which really needed drastic condemnation. Dickens effectively condemned them and they had to close.

There was no national system of compulsory schooling until 1870. Before that there were dames' schools like that kept along with a shop by Mr. Wopsle's great-aunt in *Great Expectations*. The children there paid twopence a week and somehow learned to spell. One type of urban school is derided in *Hard Times*. It is kept by a Mr. McChoakum-child whose notion of teaching is the injecting of facts and then more facts. This was much approved by the harsh employers of labour who wanted nothing gay or fanciful to distract their workers from the real business of life, which was making money for their masters.

There is, however, one exception to the Dickens denunciation of vile or stupid schooling. That is the establishment kept by Dr. Strong described in *David Copperfield*. Also there was in fact and not in fiction a quite new school of which Dickens strongly approved. This was at Bruce Castle in North London, where there was no iron discipline, initiative in study was encouraged, and the boys had the run of a large and excellent library. But this was an isolated exception. Though Dickens had no searing school-day memories of his own his mind was haunted by the idea of juvenile prisons pretending to be schools. Undoubtedly there were such.

During the eighteen-forties there was a rush of new fee-paying Colleges for the sons of the expanding, prospering, and snobbish middle class. These parents looked down on the old grammar schools for day-boys. The tradesmen could send their sons along the road to those places. The gentry favoured the new boarding-schools which got their families off their hands in a respectable and expensive way. There was not room for all those boys in the ancient foundations of Eton, Harrow, Rugby and Winchester, and the need was met all over the country in such new schools as Cheltenham, Clifton, Marlborough, Wellington and Malvern, founded on the model of the older establishments.

Their function was to train entrants for the Army, the Church and the other professions. Dr. Thomas Arnold, who became headmaster of Rugby School in 1828, had declared his purpose of turning out scholars who were Christian gentlemen. There

Miss Dorothea Beale (1831–1906), who was a pioneer of secondary education for girls, and who founded Cheltenham Ladies' College in 1853.

(Right) Young pupils working in the junior schoolroom at Eton.

were constant services in the School Chapels. He made a great reputation and became influential as an educational pioneer, but he had to confess that he frequently failed to produce the desired type which he hoped would be both virtuous and manly. Readers of *Tom Brown's Schooldays* by Thomas Hughes, published anonymously in 1857, and of *Eric or Little by Little* (1860), written by Dean Farrar, later headmaster of Marlborough, are shown a robust and coarse life and a travesty of a civilized education. Dickens was fortunate in his father's inability to give him "a gentleman's education" of this kind.

The curriculum of the Public Schools (it is an inappropriate name since they are essentially private in nature), now much widened and improved, was then narrowly classical. There was no preparation for the new world of mechanical invention, no science, no technical training, no preparation for a business career. There was much attention paid to cricket and football; to be strenuously athletic was supposed to form character. Violent exercise was expected to divert the passions from sex to sport, and sport had prestige. At Public Schools the boy who failed at games was as much out of things as if his father had been a shopkeeper.

When it was decided that girls should share in this kind of boarding-school the social status was emphasized. At first there were few of these schools. Those who could afford it looked for a governess to teach their daughters at home. The principal idea was to turn out little ladies and not little scholars. There is a remarkable example of the genteel governess in Mrs. General, whom Mr. Dorrit employed when he came into money. She thought that pronunciation was what mattered most. The girls were not to say "Father". "Papa is a preferable form of address. Father is vulgar. The word Papa gives a pretty form to the lips. Papa, potatoes, poultry, prunes and prism are very good words for the lips, especially prunes and prism." Mrs. General also insisted that it was unladylike to have any opinions or to know about anything disagreeable. "A truly refined mind will seem to be ignorant of the existence of anything which is not proper, placid, and pleasant." The business of a girl thus educated—and there were many of them—was to keep her brain inactive and her lips pursed. The world described by Dickens was far from being proper, placid and pleasant. But young ladies were to hear nothing of reality while they murmured "prunes and prism" to shape their mouths

A contemporary print of Rugby School from the south-west, with pupils playing in the grounds.

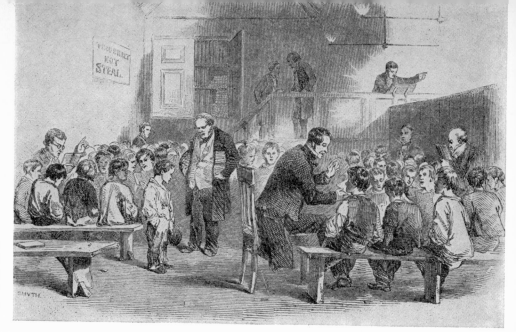

Lambeth Ragged School in 1846. Dickens wrote to the editors of the Daily News *about this attempt to educate the really poor who couldn't ever gain admission to a charity school.*

correctly before they entered a polite drawing-room. However, the climate was changing. For instance, in 1850 Miss Buss started the North London Collegiate School for Girls, a model for girls' day-schools, and three years later Miss Beale founded Cheltenham Ladies College on the same lines as a boys' Public School.

Dickens never had the chance of a University career and would have despised the Oxford and Cambridge of the years in which he might have worn a gown. Then their administration was completely dominated by the Church of England. Only members of that Church were allowed in until 1854. The Fellows of the Colleges, who did the teaching, had to be in holy orders and remain unmarried. Money permitting, Dickens could have entered University College in London which had been founded in 1828 to provide "an equality with the ancient Universities freed from exclusions and religious distinctions". He might have preferred to educate himself, as he so triumphantly did.

During his American visit of 1842 Dickens met the kind of University and a type of scholar whom he admired. The Universities, he wrote in his *American Notes*, "rear no bigots, never interpose between the people and their improvements, exclude no man because of his religious opinions, and in all their course of study and instruction, recognize a world and a broad one, lying beyond the College walls." At Harvard the professors "would shed a grace upon and do honour to any society in the civilized world". He did not visit Yale, where there was an early development of scientific studies. No doubt his approval would have been no less warm. During most of his lifetime Oxford and Cambridge were isolated relics of an old and narrow tradition. He himself had been introduced to the classics and read Virgil at thirteen with the tuition of the Latin master whom he remembered with respect. But he soon abandoned these studies to become a ready pupil in the school of life in which he learned all he needed for his novels.

42

Emigrants to Sydney in 1844 eating dinner amidships. As the quality of life and the number of jobs diminished in English villages, many families chose to seek their fortune abroad rather than in the over-crowded streets of London or the towns of the industrial North of England.

THE SAYING that "Trade follows the flag" is less true than its converse in the history of the British Empire which became the British Commonwealth. The British navy was enlarged and busily engaged in protecting trade routes where the pioneering had been done for a long time by merchant adventurers. In some cases the Christian missionaries were first in the field. Their hazardous journeys and settlements were planned to spread the Gospel and save souls, but there were material results since they, like the traders, needed protection though they were not asking for occupation by force. What was urgently required for re-fitting and re-fuelling ships was a chain of harbours across the world at places like Gibraltar, Malta, Aden, Colombo, and so on to Hong Kong. During Dickens's lifetime these links were steadily increased. Another pressure was that of Britain's rapidly increasing population. Emigration mounted and colonial careers made fortunes for the fortunate and provided work for the poor who wanted a larger life than could be found at home.

In what has been called "the scramble for Africa" Britain had an important share with the Dutch, French, Germans and Portuguese. The Cape Colony was founded before Dickens was born. The Gold Coast, now Ghana, was finally turned into a British settlement in 1850. The thrust went on in the Far East. Singapore was purchased by the British East India Company from a local ruler in 1819 and the Malay States later proved a most valuable source of rubber and tin. The Chinese market was tapped when Hong Kong was ceded by China in 1841. Not only the British were enriched. The native chiefs and sultans soon discovered that the arrival of the trader could bring advantage to all, a fact realized later by the Middle Eastern rulers of oil-rich lands.

In Victorian times there was far more penetration by commerce than by use of arms.

43

(Above) A flogging whip. Its use as punishment for breaches of discipline in the army was prohibited in 1881.

The helmet of an officer in the Sixth Dragoon Guards c. 1854.

Britain had only a small army. This was added to by raising native troops. But it could not afford to send expeditionary forces far and wide. "No great country, except English-speaking America, has been so utterly civilian in thought and practice as Victorian England", wrote G. M. Trevelyan, the eminent historian, adding that service in the army was regarded as disgraceful by the working classes. The British people remembered the use of sabre-carrying cavalry at St. Peter's Fields in Manchester in 1819 when a working-class meeting was violently dispersed in what became known as "The Battle of Peterloo". The mass of the British people described by Dickens were not infected by militarism. But they remembered Napoleon and kept an eye on France.

How then was even a small moderate army raised? There was no conscription, but extreme poverty drove men to enlist. Officers came from the nobility and middle-class with their commissions bought for them. There was colour in their uniforms, but no adventure in their lives for a while. The peace which followed the Napoleonic Wars seemed likely to last a long time. But the "death or glory" challenge came with the Crimean War (1853–56) and it evoked the dashing gallantry of the Light Brigade at Balaclava. It also demonstrated the truth of Bernard Shaw's quip made by General Burgoyne, the Georgian wit in "The Devil's Disciple": "The British soldier can stand up to anything except the British War Office."

On the shores of the Black Sea courage was frustrated by administrative chaos. The provision of supplies was grossly bungled. The delays and confusions were appalling. Medical services were utterly and cruelly inadequate. Reform was attempted on the spot by the undaunted Florence Nightingale (1820–1910), the Lady of the Lamp who strove to cope with the agonies of the sick and wounded in the overcrowded, ill-equipped premises that passed for hospitals. Florence Nightingale had trained as a nurse at a time when it was unheard of for an educated woman to take up nursing. After her return from the Crimea she founded the Nightingale Training School for Nurses which set a new standard of discipline and skill which established nursing as an acceptable profession for young women. Later she indignantly turned her revealing light on the War Office in London, exposing its sloth and ineptitude, harrying the Secretary of State, Sidney Herbert, to make radical improvements in the hospitals and barracks at home. When she had reformed the Army Medical Service she set to work on the War Office itself. But Herbert was tired, ill, and dying. The military bureaucracy was stubborn and was not going to be pushed about by a woman.

The creation of a new British Army had to wait for Edward Cardwell whom Gladstone appointed to the War Office in 1868. The selling of commissions was abolished. An age was set for the compulsory retirement of senior officers, and the infantry was completely reorganized. The chaotic mismanagement of the Crimean War naturally stimulated Dickens's contempt for officialdom and produced his withering satire in *Little Dorrit* on the job-holding Tite Barnacles and the Office of Circumlocution. That book began to appear in serial form at the end of 1855 when the Crimean scandals were being exposed.

Although Dickens's father was in the Navy Pay Office the son paid small attention to the Royal Navy in his fiction. But the Admiralty was not so sluggish as the War Office in adapting its methods and armament to a different world. Owing to great changes in the construction of ships there was constant development and innovation. The first steam-driven warship was being built in 1814, but for a long time these vessels had sails as well as engines. A typical example is that of a battleship called *Ajax III*. She had fought under sail in the Napoleonic Wars and survived to take part in the Crimean War. By then she had been one of the first of the naval vessels to be fitted with a screw propeller and steamed to the Black Sea carrying sixty guns. Armour-plating was introduced in 1854 and the first battleship known as an ironclad was launched in 1860. There followed in 1862 the development of the turret-ship which could use its guns in all directions and did not depend on the old broad-side bombardment. The turret-ships were defended by armour-plating of ten to fourteen inches thick. Lighter, swifter, and less protected cruisers were soon to follow.

(Above) A set of army surgeon's implements, terrifying in their crude simplicity.

The most memorable of Dickens's sailors is Captain Cuttle in *Dombey and Son*. He was of the Merchant Navy and is described as having been "a pilot or a skipper or a privateersman", presumably in the Napoleonic wars. The privateer was a privately owned ship which was offered to the Government and armed to help in the capture of the enemy's merchant shipping. With the end of hostilities it returned to its private business.

During the Indian Mutiny (1857–58) a British army of 40,000 was confronted with a population of 100,000,000. It held out and the revolt was checked by Generals Havelock and Campbell who relieved the besieged cities of Cawnpore and Lucknow. An important result of the Mutiny was the ending of the rule of a sub-continent by the British East India Company—a private trading company originally established under Royal Charter by Queen Elizabeth I. A Secretary of State in London presided over the new India Office in 1858 and the Indian Civil Service began its long and valuable

Florence Nightingale in the hospital at Scutari, February 1855.

administration of the sub-continent. There was no more fortune-hunting by the wealthy British merchants, known at home as Nabobs, and no more scandals of peculation.

The clash of English and French in Canada and the quarrels between the separate Canadian Provinces became acute at the time of Queen Victoria's accession. Lord Durham, whose zeal for reform at home had earned him the title of "Radical Jack", went out to Canada as Governor-General in 1838. His report, issued in 1839, brought about the Union of Upper and Lower Canada and the creation of a common legislative Assembly responsible to the Executive Council. The liberalism of Durham was of immense value in providing the way to a considerable degree of national unity and so to Dominion status. Dickens and his wife were in Canada in 1842. He went as a sight-seer and honoured guest. They saw Niagara Falls, were soaked in spray, and were delighted. At Montreal they took part in amateur theatricals before the Governor-General. It was all pleasure and no politics, but they were seeing the new Canada in the making. One of their sons later went to Canada and had a career in the Mounted Police.

In the decade between 1850 and 1860 there were important developments in Australia. Some fortunes were made in the gold-rushes which began in 1851. These brought an influx of adventurous men who liked to take the law into their own hands especially in the matter of landholdings. The population of the continent rose rapidly, but there were constitutional as well as economic advances. The separate colonies were now granted their own parliaments. Edward Cardwell (1813–86), who was Secretary of State for the Colonies before he went to do his reforming work at the War Office, put an end to the transportation of prisoners from England; thus was ended an old nuisance humiliating to Australia. At the end of *David Copperfield* Dickens sent Mr. Micawber to enjoy an unlikely success (and even to send money home) as a Magistrate and person of consequence in the imagined Australian settlement of Port Middlebay. There too he deposited the once wretched usher Mr. Mell as a headmaster. Evidently Dickens regarded Australia as the right place for happy endings.

A convivial party of French and English soldiers in the camp of the Fourth Dragoon Guards in the Crimea in 1854.

New Zealand, previously administered by the New Zealand Company under Royal Charter, received new status and constitutional freedom through an Act of the British Parliament passed in 1852. Though the native Maoris were mostly friendly there still remained a hostile section of their race. Two wars were fought before total agreement was reached and the Maoris were granted Parliamentary seats of their own. It was a lasting settlement. A new prosperity came, as in Australia, with the discovery of gold in 1861. The many Scottish immigrants helped to develop the staple industry of sheep-farming and the country, despite the handicaps of distance, isolation, and a small population, moved on to prosperity. The Empire in all its outposts had the teething-troubles of young democracies and gradually overcame them.

The British Imperialism of a noisy and "Jingo" type came later in the final phase of

Melbourne in the 1860s. The Cathedral is "Old St. Paul's", which was pulled down in 1880 when Melbourne's rapidly increasing population made the erection of a larger Anglican Cathedral necessary.

47

Victorian self-confidence. Apart from his early Canadian tour, Dickens was little concerned with the colonies which were outgrowing that soon-to-be-resented name. He sailed west and never east. He enjoyed travel in France and Italy. He made no journeys to Africa or Asia. The state of the nation at home and the fight with internal poverty and injustice gave him his principal topics. He covered a multitude of subjects and problems. In his lifetime, not long by our standards, he could not cope with more.

The reforms for which Dickens fought came slowly. They could only be achieved by passing new laws in Parliament which officials had to make effective. But Parliament he had called "the great Dust-Heap at Westminster"; he mocked its members and he scorned the Civil Service whose task it was to turn legislation into practice. Thus he made enemies where he needed willing allies. Tact was not his strong point. His great service was to impress a huge number of readers with the ugly facts of misery and injustice while he held them with the splendour of his fiction. He knew that his public had to be entertained if they were also to be instructed. His novels and journalism were directed to that double purpose.

He was too busy and too impatient to do the drudgery of sitting on committees, drafting reports and formulating Parliamentary measures in detail. His task was to make people ashamed of the social evils, to dispel their apathy and arouse their indignation. This he continually and effectively did. Others could organize: he could stimulate. So improvement came at last, even from the Dust-Heap of his derision. He had altered the climate of opinion by the compelling power of his stories.

He died exhausted and perhaps disappointed; but he had made his mark on the British way of life as no other novelist has ever done. What he wrote was immediately acclaimed and survives in undiminished appreciation. What he hoped has been gradually realized. He made a happier world with his art and a better one with his anger.

The frontispiece of the third episode of The Posthumous Papers of the Pickwick Club, *which was published in monthly numbers from April 1836 to November 1837. This is the work through which many people first come to know and love Dickens's writings.*

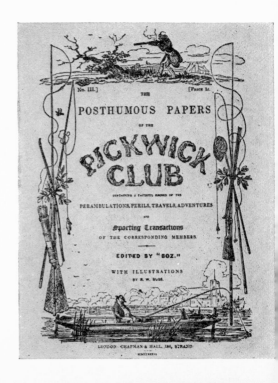